THE
SHIVA SUTRAS

Eternal Wisdom for Life

Reprint 2023

FiNGERPRINT!

An imprint of Prakash Books India Pvt. Ltd

113/A, Darya Ganj,
New Delhi-110 002,
Email: info@prakashbooks.com/sales@prakashbooks.com

`facebook` www.facebook.com/fingerprintpublishing
`twitter` www.twitter.com/FingerprintP
www.fingerprintpublishing.com

ISBN: 978 93 8917 820 3

Processed & printed in India

To the brave Kashmiri Pandits,
who preserved this ancient text for the
benefit of all mankind.

Shankarpal – the stone on which the Shiva Sutras were inscribed

CONTENTS

Introduction
7

CHAPTER ONE
Removing the Veil
13

CHAPTER TWO
Detaching from
the Body
47

CHAPTER THREE
Awakening
61

Bibliography
135

The Sutras
138

Introduction

The *Shiva Sutras* are aphorisms which, as per the legend, were revealed by Lord Shiva to the sage Vasugupta in the eighth century AD. There are three versions of how this came about. The first version says that Lord Shiva appeared to Vasugupta in a dream and revealed the *Shiva Sutras* to him. Another version says that an enlightened person revealed the sutras to Vasugupta. The third and most popular version is that Lord Shiva appeared to Vasugupta in a dream and instructed him to go to a particular stone piece. He was told that there was an esoteric teaching under the stone, and he was to study it and reveal it to those who are fit for grace. Vasugupta did as he was told the next morning, and on touching the stone, the stone turned over, and on its face were inscribed the *Shiva Sutras*. After Vasugupta studied the sutras, the stone turned back over.

The stone still exists. It is called Shankarpal, and it is located in a stream in Dachigam National Park, which is situated outside Srinagar. It is lying face down, so we do not know if anything is still written on it.

Some scholars believe that the *Shiva Sutras* spread the philosophy of Kashmir Shaivism in the region of Kashmir at the end of the eighth century, or beginning of the ninth century AD. Kashmir Shaivism was originally known as the Trika System. It is a form of yoga and tantra that is non-dualistic. Non-dualism teaches that there are not two, there is only One. The individual is not separate from God. We are all a part of one Supreme Being, who in this philosophy is usually called Paramshiva (Supreme Shiva). Sometimes it is only Shiva. Other words are also used to describe Ultimate Reality.

If we are all one, then what we are seeing in this world is not real. We appear to be separate from other beings and from other objects. We also believe that we are separate from God. This is what most religions teach. Religions tend to be dualistic. They teach separation—separation from one another and separation from God. At the end of our life we are judged by God, and we are sent to heaven and hell depending on how 'good' or 'bad' we have been.

In non-dualism, at the end of our life we all go back to God because there is nowhere else to go. There is only God or Shiva, and nothing else exists.

There are some questions that now arise. If we are all One, then why do we appear separate? What is covering our real nature? How do we get to experience our true self? What causes us to continue in the path of worldly illusion, and how do we come out of it? These are some of the issues addressed by the *Shiva Sutras*.

The sage Vasugupta is associated with two important texts of Kashmir Shaivism. The *Shiva Sutras*, which were revealed to him, and the *Spanda Karikas*, the text he authored. 'Spanda' means vibration or movement, and 'Karikas' means verses or a collection of verses. *Spanda Karikas* literally means verses on vibration. The *Spanda Karikas* explains in greater detail some of the topics discussed in the *Shiva Sutras*. It also discusses some entirely new subjects.

Both these texts belong to the Spanda System, which is one of four systems of Kashmir Shaivism. The other systems are the Kula System, the Krama System, and the Pratyabhijna System. There are two other important texts found in this system—the *Vigyan Bhairava Tantra* and the *Paratrishika*. The *Vigyan Bhairava Tantra* contains one hundred and twelve meditations for self-realization, and is probably the most important text of this system. The *Paratrishika* teaches a seed mantra that can liberate a human being in a single day.

All these texts are remarkably small but they contain an incredible wealth of information. The *Shiva Sutras* contains seventy-seven sutras, the *Spanda Karikas* consists of fifty-two verses, the *Vigyan Bhairava Tantra* has one hundred and sixty-four verses, and the *Paratrishika* has just thirty-seven verses. All the four texts complement each other and form an important part of the tradition of yoga and tantra.

The word 'sutra' literally means thread. Sometimes it is translated as 'truth' or 'directions'.

It is meant to convey a sense of essence. That it is the essence of some truth or some subject. Sutras, unlike verses, are not complete sentences. Usually it is just a phrase. Sometimes, it may only be two or three words. This creates a problem for the translator. One has to 'fill in the blanks' by adding two or three words, in order to complete a short sentence. For a few sutras, alternative meanings are possible depending on what words one adds to it. This can result in a variety of translations for a sutra. For some sutras, I have given some of the alternative possibilities, where these are important.

The *Shiva Sutras* is considered to be a little cryptic by some scholars. Actually, its message is fairly simple. Once one understands the first few sutras, the rest of the text is fairly easy to follow. We identify ourselves with our body and that is why we fail to experience the ultimate reality. This is one of the important messages of the text, which is elaborated on in a few of the sutras.

Kshemaraja wrote a commentary on the *Shiva Sutras* in the tenth century AD. He divided the seventy-seven sutras into three chapters. Since then, traditionally the *Shiva Sutras* have been divided into three chapters, although it is not necessary to do so. I have maintained the tradition of dividing the sutras into three chapters, as it makes it easier for some readers to compare this translation with earlier ones.

The *Shiva Sutras* are transformative. Once you understand them and practice them, they will open a whole new world for you.

CHAPTER ONE

Removing
the Veil

～ **1** ～

caitanyamātmā

THE SELF IS CONSCIOUSNESS.

The *Shiva Sutras* wastes no time in getting to the heart of the matter. Our true self is consciousness, not our body. The Sanskrit word *atman* is translated in two possible ways—soul and self. Both mean the same thing. The above sutra can also be translated as 'The soul is consciousness'. In spiritualism, the Self and the Soul are the same thing. The Self is the witnessing self within us that observes all our actions. When we are in a state of awareness, we are a witness, and this witness is none other than our Self or our Soul.

The word *caitanya* means consciousness. However, *caitanya* is also a technical word in Kashmir Shaivism, used for Lord Shiva. Therefore, an alternative way to translate this sutra would be: THE SELF IS SHIVA.

~§ 2 §~

jñānaṃ bandhaḥ

KNOWLEDGE CAUSES BONDAGE.

Normally we are taught that ignorance binds us and knowledge liberates us. Then, how can knowledge cause bondage? This sutra is referring to limited knowledge, not real knowledge. Limited knowledge causes us to identify with our body and not with consciousness. The previous sutra explained that our real self is consciousness. When we believe that we are the body (and not consciousness), then that belief or knowledge binds us. Why do we identify with the body? What causes us to have limited knowledge? This is explained in the next sutra.

3

yonivargaḥ kalāśarīram

THE ORIGIN OF THIS GROUP IS
THE ELEMENTS THAT CAUSE
IDENTIFICATION WITH THE BODY.

The origin of this group means the origin of people with limited knowledge. The origin of limited knowledge is caused by elements that conceal one's true nature. To understand this, we must first understand the Theory of Creation in Tantra. Ultimate Reality in Tantra is known as *Paramshiva*. Paramshiva is Supreme God or Universal Consciousness. From Paramshiva, thirty-six elements are created. From these thirty-six elements, the manifest world is created.

Paramshiva or Supreme Consciousness is present in all thirty-six elements. In Supreme Consciousness, there is some agitation or movement that causes the elements to come out. The first few elements that appear are known as the pure elements. The first element to appear is Shiva, the passive consciousness. This is followed by *Shakti*, the energy of Shiva. Then, there are three specific energies—the energy of will (*Sadashiva* or *Icchashakti*), the energy of knowledge (*Ishwara* or *Jnanashakti*), and the energy of action (*Sadvidya* or *Kriyashakti*).

After the five pure elements, the seven pure-impure elements emerge. The first six elements (elements six to eleven) are important, and they are the ones referred to in the above sutra. The sixth element is *Maya*. Maya means illusion. She veils the unity of existence and causes us to experience duality or separation. We feel separate from other objects, not one with them. In fact, there is no other object, there is only One. Maya restricts us from experiencing oneness and causes us to experience diversity.

Maya works through the next five elements, elements seven to eleven. These five elements are collectively known as *Kanchuka*. Kanchuka literally means cover. These five elements cover and conceal our true nature.

The first of these five elements (element seven) is *Kalaa*. Kalaa limits the sense of identification with Universal Consciousness to the limited individual.

Instead of identifying with consciousness, we identify with the body, or with the name and form.

The next element (element eight) is *Vidya* or knowledge, which reduces the omniscience of consciousness to limited knowledge. Vidya covers our all-knowing state and makes us experience limited knowledge.

Next is *Raga* or attraction. When we feel separate from other objects, attraction for some of them can arise. When there is no separation, there can be no attraction. You cannot be attracted to your own finger. You can only be attracted to something that is separate from you.

Element ten is *Kaala* or time. Kaala reduces the eternity of consciousness to past, present, and future. Instead of experiencing eternity, we experience time measured in seconds, minutes, hours, days, months, years, etc.

The last of the five elements (element eleven) is *Niyati*. Niyati causes restriction in space and form. Instead of experiencing the all-pervasiveness of our true nature, we experience ourselves in a particular space and form. Niyati is also sometimes translated as fate or destiny. It is the path an individual soul experiences in this world, subjected to time, space, and the Law of Karma.

Maya and these five elements cover our true nature and restrict our awareness of the Ultimate Reality. Instead of experiencing eternity and the omniscience, all-pervasiveness of our true nature, we identify with a name and form, and experience ourselves in a particular body, at a particular time, having a sequential set of experiences, which become past, present, and future.

The above sutra has a compound word consisting of two important words—*kalaa* and *shariram*. 'Kalaa' is the element that causes us to identify with the body and not with consciousness. 'Shariram' means body. Therefore, the sutra is saying that the origin of this group is the element that causes us to identify with the body. It is not just Kalaa but also Maya and the other four elements that cause us to identify with the body.

The first three sutras are therefore saying: the Self is Consciousness. Limited knowledge (believing we are the body) causes bondage. And the identification with the body is caused by Maya and the five elements that cover our true nature.

~ 4 ~

jñānādhiṣṭhānaṃ mātṛkā

MATRIKA GOVERNS THIS KNOWLEDGE.

Before explaining the sutra, it is important to know the balance elements of creation. We have so far covered eleven elements. The twelfth element is *purusha* or individual experience. This is followed by nature (*prakriti*). Nature has three qualities—inertia, dynamism, and balance. Each individual is a mixture of some combination of these three qualities.

Next are the three elements of the mind—*buddhi*, which is intellect or intelligence, *ahamkara*, which is ego, and *manas*, the thinking mind.

These elements of mind are followed by the five organs of perception—the sense of taste, smell, sight, touch, and hearing. Then there are the five organs of action—the vocal chords for speech, hands for handling, the feet for movement, the genital organs for reproduction, and the anus for excretion.

After this, we have the five *tanmatras*, which are the essence of the senses. Finally, there are the five gross elements—earth, water, fire, air, and ether or space.

The thirty-six elements enumerated above are the building blocks of life and are responsible for creation of the universe. The elements work through sound in creating the universe. Kashmir Shaivism teaches that the elements are found in the energy of sound, specifically in the energy found in the letters of the Sanskrit alphabets. From the sounds of the different Sanskrit alphabets, the universe is created. This is similar to what is written in the Bible. It reads:

"In the beginning was the Word, and the Word was with God, and the Word was God."—John 1:1

Word is sound. In Sanskrit, there is a common word, *shabd* used for both sound and word. Sanskrit has sixteen vowels, twenty-five consonants, four semi vowels, and four sibilants. For the purpose of explaining creation by sound, a fifth sibilant, *ksha* is added which is really a conjunction of two consonants. Therefore, the Sanskrit alphabet starts with the vowel 'a' and ends with the sibilant 'ksha'.

The sixteen vowels are said to contain the nature of Shiva. The twenty-five consonants contain the five gross elements, the five essence of the senses, the five organs of action, the five organs of perception, the three elements of the mind, nature (prakriti), and the individual (purusha).

The four semi vowels represent Maya and the other five elements that cover our nature. Finally, the five sibilants contain the three specific energies of Shiva, and Shakti, the main energy of Shiva.

What exactly is Matrika, and how does she govern this knowledge? Matrika is sometimes translated as Divine Mother, but she is a lot more than that. The collective energy or the sum total of all the energies of all the sounds found in the Sanskrit alphabets is Matrika. Verse 8 and 9 of the *Paratrishika* explain it beautifully:

Proceeding successively from the eternal 'a' and ending in 'ksha', are the sounds collectively known as Matrika, who is known to create the universe. She, in fact, is the governing power of all mantras

and knowledge, O Glorious One. That this is the
source has always been proclaimed in all the tantras.

Matrika governs knowledge of the created world because she is responsible for the creation of the world.

Modern science today states that all of existence is only vibration. It confirms what this sutra is saying.

~ 5 ~

udyamo bhairavaḥ

VIGOROUS AND CONTINUOUS
EFFORT LEADS TO GOD.

Whatever method we choose to reach God, we have to be totally committed to it. We cannot achieve liberation by being half-hearted in our attempt. Just as water vaporizes at hundred degree Celsius, in the same way we have to be totally committed in order to reach our goal. Our efforts must be total and continuous. Then, one day, we will awaken to a higher reality. Ramana Maharshi used to say that a fruit takes time to ripen, but a moment comes when it suddenly falls off the tree. If our efforts are vigorous and continuous, there will come a time when we will awaken to our true self in a flash.

～◦ 6 ◦～

śakticakrasaṃdhāne viśvasaṃhāraḥ

ON UNITING THE ENERGY IN THE CHAKRAS, THE UNIVERSE CEASES TO EXIST.

The literal meaning of *chakra* is wheel. It is actually an energy centre, an area where there is great concentration of energy. There are also channels (*nadis*) for allowing energy to flow in the body. There are supposed to be seventy-two thousand channels in the body. There are three that are considered to be important. The central channel (*Sushumna*), which is the main one, extends upwards through the spine. The other two are the *Ida* and the *Pingala*.

A chakra is located at the junction or meeting point of two or more channels.

There are seven important chakras. Muladhara chakra is the lowest chakra, located near the base of the spine. For men, it is located between the genital organs and the back passage. In women, it is situated at the beginning of the cervix. The next chakra is Svadhishthana chakra located above the Muladhara chakra at the base of the spine, in the region we call the tailbone. After Svadhishthana comes the Manipura chakra, which is situated in the spine, directly behind the navel. Higher up in the spine, directly behind the sternum, is the Anahata chakra. Further up in the spine, behind the throat pit, is the Vishuddha chakra. Next is the Ajna chakra, located behind the eyebrow centre. Finally, there is Sahasrara chakra, situated at the crown of the head.

The chakras and channels are not a part of the physical body; they are a part of the subtle body or energy body. If you open up the physical body, you will not find any chakras or channels. However, the subtle body controls and governs the physical body. When we have an illness, the energy flow in our body is disturbed. Certain Eastern systems of healing, such as acupuncture, attempt to balance energy flows to cure illness.

There is also the dormant energy called *kundalini*, lying in the Muladhara chakra, near the base of the spine. Many yogic practices attempt to raise this energy. When this energy rises, it moves up the central channel and pierces each chakra. When it reaches the highest chakra, that is the Sahasrara, the individual is liberated.

On uniting the energy in the chakras, the universe ceases to exist.

This sutra refers to the time when the dormant energy kundalini, situated at the base chakra, is raised to the topmost chakra. During the process, this energy unites all the chakras, and we are liberated. In a state of liberation, the universe ceases to exist. Why is this so? How does the universe disappear? The universe disappears because it is not real. When we sleep at night, we may have many dreams. Some of those dreams may seem very real. At times we may feel thirsty in the dream, at times scared, at times elated. But none of those experiences are real. When we wake up, none of the dream experiences matter. Our so-called real world is also like a dream world. When we are liberated, we awaken, and the universe in its present form ceases to exist. What we thought was the universe, we realize is none other than our Self. The Ashtavakra Gita explains it beautifully:

2.4   *Just as bubbles of foam and water*
       are not different from water,
       in the same way,
       all creation streaming out from the Self,
       is not different from the Self.

2.5   *Just as a cloth*
       may be considered to be only thread;
       like that,
       all creation may be considered to be only the Self.

2.9   *Ah, when the manifold universe appears in me,*
       it is just an illusion,
       like water shimmering in sun rays,
       a snake appearing in a strand of rope,
       or silver glistening in a sea shell.

2.10 From me the world has streamed out
and in me it will dissolve,
just like a clay pot crumbles into clay,
a wave subsides into water
and a gold bracelet melts into gold.

❧ 7 ❧

jāgratsvapnasuṣuptabhede
turyābhogasambhavaḥ

ON DIFFERENTIATING ONESELF FROM THE BODY IN THE WAKING STATE, THE DREAM STATE, AND THE STATE OF DEEP SLEEP, ONE ENJOYS THE BIRTH OF THE FOURTH STATE.

One of the fastest ways to attain liberation is to detach oneself from the body and be aware. This means that we no longer identify with the body but with consciousness. The Ashtavakra Gita says that if we are able to do this, we can be liberated immediately.

A lot of the stress and strain in life comes

because we believe we are the 'doer', the one who keeps doing things. Actually, it is our body that keeps doing things, and we are not our body. We are the witness that is aware and observes life moment to moment. This witness is the Self or the Soul.

This sutra tells us to change our perspective and whom we identify with. Instead of identifying with our body, we should identify with the witnessing Self. The sutra mentions that we differentiate ourselves from the body in the waking state, the dream state, and the state of deep sleep. Start by practicing this in the waking state. When your awareness increases, and you are nearing liberation, you will be aware even in the dream state or in deep sleep.

Some days we get stressed when we have an exceedingly busy day, and have lots of things to do. Sometimes we are also unhappy when we are doing things we do not enjoy. When we detach ourselves from the body and remain aware, our perspective and the way we experience the moment changes completely. We become peaceful even when we are busy, or doing things we do not enjoy.

Ramana Maharshi gave a wonderful example to explain this. He said that when a passenger gets onto a train with his suitcase, if he keeps the suitcase on his head, he is unnecessarily straining himself. He can put the suitcase down because the train will take him and his suitcase to the destination. In the same way, we should surrender ourselves to the Higher Power, and allow this Higher Power to work through us and lead us to our destination. When we identify with the body and believe we are the 'doer', we are unnecessarily straining ourselves, like the man carrying his suitcase on his head on the train.

⤳ 8 ⤶

jñānaṃ jāgrat

THE WAKING STATE CONSISTS OF KNOWLEDGE OF THE EXTERNAL WORLD.

The waking state is primarily concerned with the external world. Our actions and thoughts are about the external world. Our education and knowledge is also about the external world. What we call the waking state is actually also a dream state. We live in a make-believe world, where things are not what they seem. Like Alice in Wonderland, what we believe to be real is actually not so. When we truly awaken, we realize that we were living in a dream world all along.

~9 9 ~9

svapno vikalpāḥ

THE DREAM STATE IS A
VARIETY OF IMAGININGS.

When we are sleeping and dreaming, we have a variety of dreams. Our imagination becomes vivid, and our mind conjures up many different dreams.

~ 10 ~

aviveko māyāsauṣuptam

**THERE IS NO AWARENESS IN THE ILLUSORY
STATE OF DEEP SLEEP.**

In the state of deep sleep there are no thoughts and
no dreams. The state of deep sleep is similar to the
state of enlightenment, in that there are no thoughts.
However, there is one crucial difference—in deep
sleep there is no awareness. We are not aware when
we are in deep sleep.

~ 11 ~

tritayabhoktā vīreśaḥ

**ONE WHO EXPERIENCES THIS TRIAD IS
THE CHIEF OF HEROES.**

This sutra is similar to sutra 7. It is basically saying
the same thing. The triad is the three states—the
waking state, the dream state, and the state of deep

sleep. You experience this triad when you are aware during the three states. You start by being aware during the waking state. In a state of awareness, you are detached from the body and are a witness to the events unfolding in your life.

As your awareness grows, you reach a point when you are aware even during the dream state and the state of deep sleep. While dreaming, you are aware that you are dreaming. In deep sleep you are aware that you are sound asleep. The witness in you is awakened to the extent that it is never 'switched off'. At this stage you become the chief of heroes, the most heroic of all the heroes—you become enlightened.

vismayo yogabhūmikāḥ

THE DIFFERENT STAGES OF
YOGA CAUSE AMAZEMENT.

Buddha once said, 'Those who are awake live in a state of constant amazement.' The different stages of yoga result in higher and higher levels of awareness. One becomes more and more awake. Becoming awake changes your whole world. You experience things you have never experienced before. You look at life in a whole new way. You see beauty in places you had overlooked. You may appreciate the colour of a flower, or an article of clothing. There is a feeling of joy that fills you and flows out of you. This is because you have come in touch with your Highest Self. There is a deep sense of gratitude for what you have been given. You live in amazement at the beauty of life, and all your problems seem trivial and unimportant.

One experiences great peace in a heightened state of awareness. When the noise of the mind is shut down, the beauty of life suddenly becomes apparent. You are amazed at the beauty and wonder of life and at how joyful life can be.

∼ **13** ∼

icchā śaktir umā kumārī

THE POWER OF DESIRE IS THE GODDESS, CONSORT OF SHIVA.

One of the topics emphasized in the *Spanda Karikas* is the power of desire. Verses 33-36 explain this:

> *According to the desire abiding in the heart, God brings about creation of what has been desired. This is what causes the sun and moon to reach its end, resulting in awakening of the embodied.*

> *So, even in the dream state, from a continuous request for one's desire, God who is always abiding in the centre of oneself, will certainly manifest most vividly, the objects that are desired.*

Otherwise, one may be giving up the freedom to create, which is the nature of God that is constantly with one, as is the case of ordinary people in both the waking and dream state.

Since initially one's goal manifests unclearly. However, on constant attention of the mind on it, the object is made to manifest most clearly through the continuous exercise of one's power.

The *Shiva Sutras* show the importance of desire in achieving our goal by elevating the power of desire to the level of a Goddess. Desire is a very important creation tool that helps us achieve our goals, whether spiritual or material.

~ 14 ~

dṛśyaṃ śarīram

THE ENTIRE WORLD IS ONE'S OWN BODY.

The entire world is part of one Supreme Being, who we normally refer to as God or Shiva. We are part of this same Being. Therefore, by extension, this entire world is a part of us and is like one's own body. There is only One Supreme Energy that we are all part of. Everything in the world is interconnected and is part of this Supreme Being.

There is a term called *Kaivalya* used to describe the state of enlightenment. Kaivalya also means that we are alone. In a state of enlightenment, you realize that there is only one, there is only you, and nothing else exists. A similar term, Kevali, is used later in the text (sutra 34 of chapter three), to describe the liberated state. It is meant to convey the sense of oneness and aloneness. That you alone exist. This 'you', of course, in the liberated state is God.

hṛdaye cittasaṃghaṭṭād dṛśyasvāpadarśanam

FROM FOCUSING THE MIND ON THE HEART, THE WORLD APPEARS AS A DREAM.

Focusing the mind on the heart is a meditation practice. Once you practise this successfully, you become liberated and the world appears as a dream. The world appears as a dream simply because after liberation, the true nature of the world is realized. The world is not real. Once you truly awaken, you realize you were living in a dream world all along.

There is a story that will explain this. When it is dark, we might mistake a rope for a snake and become scared. But in light, we realize that it is only a rope and there is nothing to be afraid of. The external world is somewhat like this. We might experience fear in our daily lives. But when we are liberated, we realize that the world is not real, and there is nothing to be afraid of. Fear is completely absent from the life of a liberated person.

The meditation practice is given in verse 49 of the *Vigyan Bhairava Tantra*:

When the senses are absorbed in the inner space of the heart, one should concentrate with undivided attention on the centre of the two bowls of the lotus, located there. Then, O Beloved, one obtains the Supreme Fortune.

～ **16** ～

śuddha-tattva-saṃdhānād vā 'paśuśaktiḥ

OR FROM JOINING WITH THE PURE STATE, ONE OBTAINS DIVINE ENERGY.

The Pure State is the state of Consciousness. Once you remain aware, your thoughts diminish, and ultimately stop completely. That is when you reach the highest state of awareness and obtain Divine Energy. The *Vigyan Bhairava Tantra* explains in verse 62:

When the mind has left a thought and is restrained from moving towards another thought, it comes to rest in the middle. Then, through that middle state of being, one's true nature blossoms brilliantly.

It further goes on to state in verse 108:

O Deer-eyed One, by stopping all thoughts, the mind will be without support. Then the self will become the Supreme Self of God.

~ **17** ~

vitarka ātmajñānam

DELIBERATION LEADS TO KNOWLEDGE OF THE SELF.

The word 'vitarka' means deliberation, reflection. What does one deliberate or reflect on? And how does it lead to knowledge of the Self? One deliberates on the Self. One asks oneself the question, "Who am I?" This is a method made famous by Ramana

Maharshi in the first half of the twentieth century. Although the *Shiva Sutras* were revealed in the eighth century, and Ramana Maharshi lived in the twentieth century, there are many similarities in their teachings.

Ramana Maharshi called his method a process of self-enquiry. Every time a thought arises, one should ask oneself the question, "Who am I? Whom do these thoughts belong to?" The mind is nothing but our ego. It causes us to identify with the body. It is only a bundle of thoughts, and has no permanent existence. The thoughts arise because there is a thinker. The thinker is the ego. When we seek its origin, it disappears by itself, and then all that is left is the Self.

Ramana Maharshi called this a direct method for self-realization. He compared the ego to an uninvited guest in a wedding party. When the uninvited guest is sought for, the guest sensing trouble, quickly disappears. The mind or the ego is just like that. When we seek their source, they also disappear.

18

lokānandaḥ samādhisukham

THE JOY OF LIBERATION IS BLISS
FOR THE WHOLE WORLD.

All things are connected. We are all part of one Whole. What happens in one part of the world affects people and influences events in another part of the world. A person who is liberated impacts the entire world in a positive way. Their joy is felt in the entire world. A liberated person's energy rises to a very high plane, to the level of bliss. This affects the energy of all other forms in the world. The energy of the great masters such as Krishna, Buddha, and Christ brings joy to millions of people, even centuries after they have passed away.

∾ **19** ℀

śaktisandhāne śarīrotpattiḥ

ON UNITING WITH ENERGY, ONE GAINS THE ABILITY TO LEAVE THE BODY.

The last few sutras of this chapter deal with the powers a person gains once they are liberated. Uniting with Energy means that one has united with God. One's soul or spirit can then consciously leave the body, either for a short period or permanently. One gains the ability to do this at will.

∾ **20** ℀

bhūtasaṃdhāna-bhūtapr̥thaktva-viśvasaṃghaṭṭāḥ

ONE HAS THE POWER TO JOIN ELEMENTS, OR TO SEPARATE ELEMENTS, OR TO JOIN EVERYTHING.

One gains mastery of all the elements, which are the building blocks of matter. One is able to create new objects by joining elements. One is able to cure diseases by separating elements. One is also able to see the true reality of everything, joined together in one Whole.

~❧ 21 ❧~

śuddhavidyodayācckreśatva-siddhiḥ

THROUGH THE APPEARANCE OF PURE KNOWLEDGE, ONE ATTAINS MASTERY OF THE CHAKRAS.

Pure knowledge appears when one has self-realized and reached one's highest state. At that time, one acquires mastery of the chakras, or energy centres in the body. When you acquire mastery of the chakras, your entire body gets revitalized. The body is nothing but an energy system, and the chakras are what control the energy in your body. Once you gain control of the chakras, you are effectively able to control the health of your body.

22

mahāhradānusaṃdhānānmantravīry ānubhavaḥ

FROM UNION WITH THE GREAT LAKE, ONE GAINS THE POWER OF MANTRA.

The great lake is a reference to Lord Shiva, the great pool of consciousness. When you unite with God you gain the power of mantra. Mantras are sounds that generally raise one's level of consciousness. They all have a creative force in them and can bring about a specific result, such as improvement in health, intelligence, and so on. The important mantras contained the elements of creation, and were responsible for the creation of the Universe and all forms in it.

This sutra is simply trying to state that on liberation one becomes a Creator and gains the creative power of mantra.

CHAPTER TWO

Detaching
from the Body

The ten sutras contained in this chapter are significant. They hold an important message about the nature of the mind and body and the means to fulfilment.

～ 1 ～

cittaṃ mantraḥ

MANTRA STILLS THE MIND.

We need to still the mind in order to self-realize or unite with God. This is something all important texts of yoga state. The *Vigyan Bhairava Tantra* in verse 15 mentions that we experience the bliss of God within ourselves when the mind is still and free of thoughts. Patanjali's *Yoga Sutras* states in the second and third sutras that when the mind is stilled, we reside in our natural state.

Mantras are special sounds that have the ability to awaken us to a higher reality. Some of the important mantras were heard by the ancient sages when they were deep in meditation.

A mantra may or may not mean something. The meaning of a word in a mantra is not important. It is the sound of the mantra that is important. Take the example of the famous mantra 'Om Namah Shivaya.' The literal meaning is Salutations to Shiva. However, Om Namah Shivaya consists of seven syllables—Om, Na, ma, h, Shi, va, ya. Each of these seven syllables stimulates one of the seven important chakras, and thereby raises consciousness.

Some of the most important mantras are *bija* mantras or seed mantras. They typically consist of a single word. Om or AUM is a seed mantra. In Kashmir Shaivism, the most important seed mantra is the mantra 'Sauh', given in the important text *Paratrishika*.

Usually a mantra is given to you by a Guru. The Guru gives a mantra specifically for you, which he thinks is most suited for raising your level of consciousness. Most mantras, including Om Namah Shivaya, should only be practiced under the guidance of a Guru.

One of the most important mantras for liberation is the sound of one's breath. Listening to the sound of one's breath quickly stills the mind. At the end of

112 meditations in the *Vigyan Bhairava Tantra,* Lord Shiva gives one more meditation. A meditation he considered important and through which it was easy to attain success. This meditation is listening to the sound of one's breath.

2

prayatnaḥ sādhakaḥ

PERSEVERING EFFORT LEADS TO FULFILMENT.

Whatever Sadhana or spiritual practice we choose, we must persevere in it. It could be a particular meditation, or a mantra, or some other practice. Whatever it may be, we should be determined to continue with it. Too often, we let the problems of our daily life interrupt our practice. We get caught up in the drama of our lives and lose focus. When you become overly concerned with the outer reality, it becomes more difficult to still the mind. Masters know that life resolves itself in the process of life itself. Problems get resolved in due course. Every day new problems arise and old problems get resolved. It is important to have trust in God and faith in the process of life. We should surrender to the Divine. God makes the world and is perfectly capable of looking after us.

When we still the mind and live in awareness, we live one moment at a time. When we encounter a problem, we know intuitively the first step to be taken to resolve the problem. Our soul brings us far greater wisdom than our mind. When we live outside our mind, situations are no longer problems. Something is just what it is. It is our mind that colours it negatively, passes judgment, and creates fear.

~ 3 ~

vidyāśarīra-sattā mantrarahasyam

KNOWLEDGE ON THE REALITY OF THE BODY IS THE SECRET OF MANTRA.

Mantras are composed of sounds and letters. These sounds and letters contain energy and the elements of creation. It is these elements of creation that are responsible for the creation of matter, including the body. The body is created by these elements of creation found in certain sounds or mantras.

A detailed description of the Theory of Creation in Tantra is given at the beginning of the text in the commentary to sutras 3 and 4.

~~ **4** ~~

garbhe cittavikāso 'viśiṣṭavidyāsvapnaḥ

IN THE INTERIOR OF THE ACTIVE MIND IS FOUND INFERIOR KNOWLEDGE OF THE DREAM WORLD.

Our thinking mind and brain contains knowledge of the external world. This external world is not real, it is like a dream world. Knowledge of the dream world is considered inferior because it is knowledge about something that is not real. It is also the knowledge that can bind us. We look at the world with its different forms, and we believe that all the forms are separate. We also believe that we are the particular form called our body. Our beliefs prevent us from experiencing higher reality. They need to be changed for us to awaken.

~ 5 ~

vidyāsamutthāne
śvābhāvike khecarī śivāvasthā

ON RAISING OF KNOWLEDGE INHERENT IN ONESELF, ONE REACHES THE HIGHEST STATE OF CONSCIOUSNESS, WHICH IS THE STATE OF SHIVA.

Raising of knowledge inherent in oneself refers to Kundalini, the dormant energy situated in Muladhara chakra. When we raise the energy up through the spine, it pierces each chakra. When it reaches the topmost chakra, the Sahasrara chakra, we become fully liberated. We attain the highest level of consciousness, which is the state of Shiva. We fully realize and experience our oneness with God or Shiva.

The question now arises, how does one raise the energy that is inherent in oneself? This text gives a few methods for doing so.

∼⋟ 6 ⋞∼

gururupāyaḥ

THE GURU IS THE MEANS.

∼⋟ 7 ⋞∼

mātṛkācakrasambodhaḥ

FOR AWAKENING THE ENERGY IN THE CHAKRAS.

One way to raise the energy that is within us is to go to a Guru who knows the methods for doing so. In ancient times, there were always some liberated masters. One had to approach them and request them to accept you as their disciple. Once you became their disciple, they would teach you over time how to raise your level of consciousness and become enlightened.

Is it absolutely necessary to have a Guru in order to attain self-realization? Or is it possible to achieve liberation without an external Guru? There are some traditions which maintain that an external Guru is necessary, and without one, one will not be able to achieve liberation. There are others who disagree. Ramana Maharshi achieved liberation without the help of any Guru. He used to say that the highest Guru is the one within us. The role of the external Guru is to introduce you to the internal Guru. Because we mistakenly think we are the body, we also believe the external Guru is their body. Actually, there is only one Self or Soul within us that encompasses us and the Guru. The best thing we can do for our evolution is to listen to the Self within us. That Source within will sometimes lead us to an external Guru, when it is beneficial for our evolution to learn from that Guru. At other times, the right book may be placed in our hands, or a chance remark from a friend may move our evolution forward. It is important, therefore, to never ignore the voice within us, or the wisdom within us that comes from the highest source.

Having said that, having an external Guru, specially a realized master, can make a huge difference to the speed of our evolution. A Guru has walked the path. They have covered territory that is still unknown to us. Having them lead us can be of immense help. When we enter unknown territory, we can sometimes lose our way. But someone who knows the path, will hold our hand and lead us to our destination. It is for this reason, this text emphasizes the importance of a Guru. Without a Guru, we can still attain enlightenment. But it will take longer and take more effort. A Guru knows the way and can take us more rapidly to a liberated state.

8

śarīraṃ haviḥ

THE BODY IS THE SACRIFICE.

9

jñānam annam

KNOWLEDGE IS FOOD TO BE CONSUMED.

vidyāsaṃhāre taduttha-svapna-darśanam

ON DESTRUCTION OF THIS KNOWLEDGE, ONE AWAKENS FROM EXPERIENCING THE DREAM STATE.

The three sutras need to be read together. These sutras have puzzled people over the centuries, but when read together their meaning becomes clear. One does not physically sacrifice the body. One destroys the idea that I am the body. This is the knowledge that causes bondage. This false knowledge, 'I am the body', is to be destroyed. This knowledge is to be consumed like food, so that it no longer exists.

Our identification with our body causes our bondage. These three sutras are asking us to destroy this belief. Once we remove identification with name and form, then all that is left is awareness. We then awaken out of the dream state.

The Ashtavakra Gita makes the remarkable statement in its first few verses, that if we can set the body aside (give up believing we are the body), and rest in awareness, we will be free at once. Nisargadatta Maharaj used to say that liberation is never of the person, it is always from the person. It is when we stop identifying with the name and form that we become liberated.

The *Vigyan Bhairava Tantra* gives quite a few meditations for removing identification with the body. There is one where you visualize a fire starting from the right toe of the body, rising upwards and destroying the body. When the body is destroyed, there is only awareness. There are others where you imagine the body is like an empty shell with nothing inside. All these meditations raise our level of awareness by changing our beliefs and removing attachment with the body.

CHAPTER THREE

Awakening

~ 1 ~

ātmā cittam

THE INDIVIDUAL SELF IS THE MIND.

In yoga, the mind and the body together constitute the ego. The mind and the body are connected. You have the physical body and the mental body. The mind causes us to identify with the body and with the name and form. The mind is responsible for creating our limited sense of self. That I am this particular individual, with this name, having this particular body. Our sense of individuality, being a particular person, is our ego and is caused by the mind. That is why there is so much importance laid on stilling the mind. It is only when we still the mind that we go beyond our limited self and experience our higher self.

The first three sutras of this chapter should be compared with the first three sutras of chapter one. The first sutra of chapter one says that the Self is Consciousness. Our real self is consciousness, not our body and mind. The first sutra here says that our individual self is the mind.

~∞ 2 ∞~

jñānaṃ bandhaḥ

KNOWLEDGE CAUSES BONDAGE.

This sutra is a repetition of the second sutra of chapter one. Certain important messages are repeated throughout the book. Limited knowledge causes bondage. Knowledge acquired through the mind can also cause bondage. The mind tends to separate, to divide. It sees separate forms, separate individuals. It creates beliefs that reinforce the sense of separateness. The belief that we are the body causes bondage.

Vasugupta explains some of the text of the *Shiva Sutras* in greater detail in the *Spanda Karikas*. This is what he says in verses 49 and 50 of the *Spanda Karikas*:

Due to the appearance of the body, consisting of the five subtle elements, one believes that they are the body. Abiding in the perception that one is the eight constituent parts of the body hinders the appearance of one's true state. The existence of this belief

Causes one to become subservient to the sensory pleasures. For this reason, one experiences mundane existence. Now, we will explain the means for ending this mundane existence.

~๑ **3** ๑~

kalādīnāṃ tattvānām aviveko māyā

THE ILLUSION IS CAUSED BY THE INABILITY TO DISCERN THE NATURE OF ELEMENTS, BEGINNING WITH THE ELEMENTS OF CONCEALMENT.

We live in an illusory world, like Alice in Wonderland, where things are not what they seem. Our world has multiple life forms, some animate and some inanimate. Each form seems separate from the other. Each seems to have a 'birth' and a 'death'. Yet every master says we are all one. Our bodies may pass away, but there is only one soul encompassing all our bodies, which is eternal. We may look separate, but there is only one life force breathing life into our bodies.

What causes the illusion? The illusion is caused by certain elements of creation, which cover and conceal our true nature. These elements are described in detail in the commentary to sutra 3 of the first chapter.

The first element of concealment is Maya. Maya means illusion. Maya veils the unity of existence and causes us to experience separation. It works through the following five elements—

1) Kalaa, which causes us to identify with the body and not with Universal Consciousness.

2) Vidya (knowledge), which conceals our omniscience and makes up experience-limited knowledge.

3) Raga or attraction, which causes us to feel attraction towards other objects. Because we feel separate from other objects, attraction for some of them can arise. When there is no separation, there can be no attraction.

4) Kaala (time), which causes us to experience time in the form of past, present, and future, instead of experiencing eternity.

5) Niyati, which causes restriction in space and form. Our true self is all-pervasive. Niyati causes us to experience ourselves in a particular space and form.

All these elements create the illusion. When we are able to discern them and look past them, we begin to experience the Ulitmate Reality. One way of doing this is to believe we are all one, even when our sense organs are showing us the opposite. There is a beautiful meditation in the *Vigyan Bhairava Tantra* (verse 110) to this effect:

> *Just as waves arise from water, flames from fire, light from the sun—in the same way, the various forms of the universe have arisen from me, God.*

Kashmir Shaivism is sometimes compared to Advaita Vedanta, the philosophy of the Upanishads. Both these philosophies are non-dualistic, and teach that we are all One. There is only one God or Being, whom we are all a part of. The division and separation appearing in the world are not real. What then is the difference between the two philosophies? According to some practitioners of Kashmir Shaivism, Advaita Vedanta teaches that the world is an illusion, whereas Kashmir Shaivism says that the world is real. This is not strictly correct. Kashmir Shaivism says that the world is real in the sense that it is created by the energy of God; but its appearance is completely unreal. It goes to great lengths to show through the Theory of Creation how some elements of creation (Maya, Kalaa, etc.) mask and conceal true reality.

The differences between these two philosophies are more to do with the practices followed to achieve enlightenment. They also use different names for God or Ultimate Reality. Advaita Vedanta uses the word Brahman for God, whereas in Kashmir Shaivism, God is Paramshiva or Shiva. Kashmir Shaivism also goes to great lengths to explain through the Theory of Creation, how the world is created and why it appears the way it does.

When we study both these philosophies, there are two words that keep coming up, which explain what is considered important for our evolution.

They are *viveka* (discrimination) and *vairagya* (detachment). Discrimination is important because we need to discriminate between what is real and what is unreal. Too often what we think is real, is actually unreal. What this sutra and some of the previous sutras are trying to do, is to show us what is unreal. They are trying to make us see through the illusion, and uncover true reality. As long as we perceive the world to be real, we will not be able to experience ultimate reality.

Detachment is considered important because when we are affected by external events, we are making the world real. One reason we find it difficult to still our mind is that we keep thinking about the world and the events affecting our life. When we understand the world is unreal, we stop giving it so much importance. We shift our focus from the world to our Self, from the unreal to the real. Detachment becomes easy when we believe the world is unreal. Why would we think about something that is unreal? Masters are those who have consciously denied the reality of the world. Even when they were being tortured or put to death, they loved their enemies. They realized that there was no separation between their enemies and them, and they were not their body. The death of their body would not affect their eternal Self.

◦❀ 4 ❀◦

śarīre saṃhāraḥ kalānām

DISSOLUTION OF THE ELEMENTS OF CONCEALMENT IN THE BODY LEADS TO,

~ 5 ~

nāḍī-saṃhāra-bhūtajaya-bhūtakaivalya-bhūtapṛthaktvāni

SUSPENSION OF BREATH IN THE CHANNELS,
CONTROL OVER THE ELEMENTS, DETACHMENT
FROM THE ELEMENTS, AND SEPARATION
FROM THE ELEMENTS.

When the elements of concealment dissolve, or are removed through our spiritual practices, we undergo certain experiences and gain supernatural powers. When our consciousness rises suddenly, our breath may get suspended. We may stop breathing for a short period of time. Ordinarily when this happens, our blood pressure would rise, but when we experience this in moments of enlightenment, there are no adverse effects on the body.

We also gain control over the elements. We are able to use the elements and create matter. We become completely detached from the elements and from our body. We no longer experience ourselves as the body but as consciousness.

mohāvaraṇāt siddhih

SUPERNATURAL POWERS ARE DUE TO A VEIL DRAWN BY DELUSION.

The word *moha*, used in this and the next sutra, can be translated as ignorance or delusion. Supernatural powers occur due to a veil drawn by ignorance or delusion.

The supernatural powers appear just before enlightenment. Patanjali, in his *Yoga Sutras*, warned that these powers are a distraction and should be ignored. If we get seduced by them, we regress in our development and soon the powers also disappear. The sutra seems to be saying the same thing. If you get seduced by the supernatural powers, it means that there is still some ego left. You feel special or different by having these powers, and using these powers gratifies your ego. This means you are still trapped by delusion or the illusion. The illusion says that you are separate, and there is now something special about you. The reality is that you are part of one Whole, and you cannot be more special when there is only One.

mohajayād anantābhogāt sahajavidyājayaḥ

FROM A COMPLETE AND ALL-PERVASIVE VICTORY OVER DELUSION, ONE GAINS THE VICTORY OF NATURAL, INNATE KNOWLEDGE OF TRUE REALITY.

Once the supernatural powers are ignored, and one continues on the spiritual path, there comes a time when the ego disappears completely. It is at that time that one gains complete victory over delusion or ignorance. What is gained by being victorious over delusion? One gains knowledge of True Reality. So far we have only acquired knowledge of the illusory world, mainly through our mind and the sense organs. Now, we acquire knowledge of True Reality. This knowledge of true reality is innate in us. It was always there within us. We have only brought it out. It is often said that the process of self-realization is one of remembrance. We had forgotten our True Self, and now we remember.

~ 8 ~

jāgrad-dvitīya-karaḥ

BECOMING AWAKE IS THE SECOND EFFECT.

Becoming awake is the second effect of being victorious over the illusion. We do not just gain knowledge of True Reality, we also experience it. We awaken from the dream world we were living in, the world we thought was so real, and we experience the Ultimate Reality.

Normally, when we sleep at night and we dream, the experiences we have while dreaming seem so real. When we are thirsty while dreaming, we feel the thirst. When we wake up in the morning, we realize that all the experiences we had while dreaming were so trivial and unreal. Something similar happens when we are liberated. We truly awaken and we realize that we were living in an illusory world. All the fears we had were actually unfounded. When we are living in this world and we think it is real, we experience fear. When we awaken to higher reality, we see the truth, and all our fears drop away.

৵৹ 9 ৹৵

nartaka ātmā

THE SELF IS AN ACTOR.

Hinduism has always held that the world is not real; it is *lila*—a play or a sport. You are like an actor on a stage. You have a role to play. Do not get affected or burdened by the role you are playing. Realize that it is not real. You can then sit back and enjoy your life with its various ups and downs. Normally, we are so burdened with the day-to-day problems we face. We try to be successful all the time. And when we happen to fail, we get upset. There are some people who even go into depression because their life did not turn out the way they wanted it to. But when we understand that we are like actors only playing a part, and that none of this is real, and none of it ultimately matters, the stress and tension in life disappears. We can then look at certain events in our life and have a good laugh instead of taking them so seriously. We also then understand that the achievements of the body do not matter to the soul.

What we define as success is different from what the soul defines as success.

The self referred to in the sutra is the individual self or the individual person. The basic message of this and the next two sutras is—do not get caught up in the role you are playing in life and make it real. Understand, it is just a role that you are acting out and none of it is real. You will then face the ups and downs of life with peace and equanimity that were not there before. You will accept good fortune and misfortune with the same peace of mind. And this change will come about simply because you have changed your perspective. When you look at things in a new way, you are no longer disturbed by the way events unfold in your life.

This sutra and the next two sutras give the same message. It is a message God has sent us through many different people at many different times. In William Shakespeare's *Merchant of Venice*, Antonio says, "I hold the world but as the world, Gratiano; A stage, where every man must play a part, and mine a sad one." Also in Shakespeare's *As You Like It*, Jacques says in Act II Scene VII, "All the world's a stage, and all the men and women merely players.

They have their exits and their entrances, and one man in his time plays many parts, his acts being seven ages."

∼ **10** ∼

raṅgo 'ntarātmā

THE INNER SELF IS THE STAGE.

The inner self referred to here is the mind. The mind creates the world, therefore the world is the stage. Ramana Maharshi used to say that just as a spider draws the thread of the web out from itself and again withdraws it into itself; in the same way, the mind projects the world out from itself, and also dissolves it back into itself. When the mind is stilled, the world as we know it disappears.

There is a beautiful passage in Neale Donald Walsch's *Conversations with God: Book 3* that expresses the same message as these sutras—"Nothing is painful which you understand is not real. It is like a movie, a drama, played out on the stage of your mind. You are creating the situation and the characters. You are writing the lines."

Although, we are playing a role in life, not everything is predestined. We do change the script through our thoughts, words, and actions.

∽ 11 ∽

prekṣakāṇi indriyāṇi

THE SENSE ORGANS ARE THE SPECTATORS.

The question may arise that if we are like actors on the stage of the world, then what is the purpose of being in this world? The purpose is evolution. To have experiences that increase our level of awareness, till we reach a state of unity with God. By seeing ourselves as actors on a stage, we do not let life affect us negatively in any way. The example of a lotus flower is given. A lotus grows in water, but if you touch it, you will find it is dry. Although, it is found in water, it does not let water affect its quality and make it wet. We apply the same lesson in our lives when we see ourselves as actors on a stage. We do not allow the world to affect us.

When we get caught up in our life story and make it real, we allow events in our life to pressurize us and make us unhappy. Then life is no longer enjoyable, and feels like a burden. There is a beautiful passage in the Ashtavakra Gita that explains this:

4.1   Look! The wise man knows the Self
       and plays the game of life.
       He is not at all comparable with the foolish,
       who carry the burden of worldly illusion.

How do we ensure that we do not get caught up in the dramas unfolding in our lives? It is similar to what happens when we watch a movie. Sometimes, we get so engrossed in a movie, we start reacting to the events being played out on the screen. The way we come out of this is by giving attention to our self. When we again focus on the fact that we are sitting in a movie theatre, the movie loses its hold on us. Similarly, in life, once we give attention to our Self, we become a witness and no longer identify with the role we are playing. External events cease to affect us, and life becomes a joy once more.

~ **12** ~

dhīvaśāt sattva-siddhiḥ

THROUGH DESIRE FOR SPIRITUAL WISDOM, ONE ATTAINS THE TRUE STATE.

Desire is the basic energy that starts the process of creation. This is true for material desires as well as spiritual ones. When you become intent on being liberated, the universe conspires in every way to make this possible. You meet the right people or the right Gurus, who help you on the way. A book might fall into your hands by chance that moves you forward in your evolution. Most of the time our desires become dissipated. We get engrossed in our day-to-day lives and lose focus on our goals. It is for this reason we make slow progress. Whatever your goals may be, if you are constantly focused, the results will be rapid. If your desire is intense, you may even become liberated within a single day.

Vasugupta in the *Spanda Karikas* gave great importance to the power of desire. He wrote a considerable number of verses on it.

This sutra echoes the famous passage in the Bible (Matthew 7:7)—"Ask, and it shall be given to you; seek and ye will find; knock, and it shall be opened unto you."

~ **13** ~

siddhaḥ svatantrabhāvaḥ

FREEDOM IS ACQUIRED.

Buddha was once asked, "What have you gained from meditation?" He replied, "Nothing." However, Buddha continued, "Let me tell you what I lost: anger, anxiety, depression, insecurity, fear of old age and death."

When you become enlightened, you acquire freedom. You are no longer bound by the illusion and become free of pain and suffering. You also become free of the afflictions mentioned by the Buddha. The basic freedom you acquire is freedom from the illusion. The illusory world no longer binds you or controls you. Your inner state of being is not influenced or controlled by external events. You also become free from the cycle of birth and death.

～♾ 14 ♾～

yathā tatra tathā anyatra

SINCE THERE, SO ELSEWHERE.

An important freedom that is acquired after liberation is that one is no longer identified with the body. As discussed earlier, there are some elements of creation that cover our true nature. They cause us to lose our all-pervasiveness, and make us believe we are limited to the body. With liberation, we break our link to the body and regain our all-pervasiveness. **Since there, so elsewhere.** Since we are in one place, we are also in every place.

Enlightenment removes the illusion of separateness. Earlier, we believed we were all separate beings in a particular place, at a particular time. With enlightenment, that illusion is removed. There is only One Being, and that Being exists everywhere.

~ **15** ~

bījāvadhānam

ATTENTIVENESS IS THE SEED.

Attentiveness is the seed that blossoms into the tree of enlightenment. Enlightenment is a state of full awareness. To reach full awareness, one first has to start with little awareness. To be attentive to the present moment, to whatever we are doing, is the beginning. Usually our mind takes us away from the present moment, to the future or to the past. When that happens, we should bring our mind back to the present moment, to the here and now, and focus completely on whatever we are doing.

In some science fiction movies, there is a portal or a gateway that transports us to another world. When we enter a portal, we are immediately transported to another world, many light years away. Sometimes in these movies, a portal allows us to travel back or forward in time.

In spirituality, the concept of a portal is a little different. A portal is something that takes us to a higher plane of existence. It can cause us to reach a higher level of awareness, and attain enlightenment. The present moment is one such portal. It is a gateway to liberation. Giving full attention to the present moment is a rapid way to achieve enlightenment. When we are fully in the present moment, and not even 1% of our attention is elsewhere, we achieve enlightenment. But it all begins by being attentive. Attentiveness is the seed.

āsanasthaḥ sukhaṃ hrade nimajjati

SITTING COMFORTABLY, ONE EFFORTLESSLY DIVES INTO AN OCEAN OF BLISS.

After reaching a certain level of awareness, when one sits for meditation, one easily moves into a state of bliss. It is like diving into an ocean of bliss, because the bliss is so overwhelming, so full, that it completely surrounds and envelops one.

Some masters have been known to go into a trance and remain there for hours. People in their presence could feel a deep sense of peace and joy emanating from them. There are other masters like Ramakrishna, who would suddenly get up and start dancing. He was in a state of ecstasy, and the ecstasy was so overwhelming that he would go into a trance and start dancing.

When you get a taste of that bliss, even for a short period of time, you come out of that experience a completely changed person. You will never want to harm any other person ever again. Nor will you need anything from anyone again.

You will know that external experiences or external events can never give you even a fraction of the joy that you experience within. This understanding will completely change the way you deal with the external world. External events will no longer influence your inner state of being. You will not require people to be nice to you, or to do things for you. Others' behaviour towards you will no longer matter. You will be so overwhelmed and grateful for the experience you have been given, that all you will want is to share it with others.

～ 17 ～

svamātrānirmāṇam āpādayati

HE CAN BRING ABOUT CREATION OF MATTER FROM HIS OWN SELF.

When you reach the level of God Consciousness, you are one with God; you are one with the Creator. At that stage you are God, and you have the ability to create matter from your own self. You are not an entity separate from God, or different from God. We are all always one with God. But our oneness has been concealed by the illusion. When we realize our true self (self-realization), we experience our oneness with God. At that stage we become the Creator, and are able to create matter.

The potential to reach a level of God Consciousness exists within all of us. Sometimes, when Jesus performed miracles, people were amazed by what he had achieved. He then said to them, "Why are you so amazed? These things and more shall you do also."

18

vidyā-avināśe janma-vināśaḥ

WHEN KNOWLEDGE OF SELF BECOMES
PERMANENT, THE POSSIBILITY OF ANOTHER
BIRTH IS COMPLETELY ELIMINATED.

People sometimes ask why we are reborn. What is the purpose of reincarnation or the cycle of birth and death? The main purpose of reincarnation is to achieve higher and higher levels of awareness, till we reach a state of full awareness, or God Consciousness. Whatever level of awareness we achieve in one lifetime, we start from that level of awareness in our next lifetime. We do not start our next lifetime from zero. In each lifetime, we raise our level of awareness to some extent. Like this, in each life cycle we keep raising our awareness till we are fully awake.

When knowledge of the Self becomes permanent, we have reached the highest level of consciousness that is possible, and are one with God. Then, the cycle of birth and death ends for us, as there is no higher level left to go. The possibility of another birth is eliminated, as the sutra says.

kavargādiṣu māheśvaryādyāḥ paśu-mātaraḥ

MAHESHWARI AND OTHER ENERGIES OF GOD, RESIDE IN THE LETTERS BEGINNING WITH THE K GROUP, AND THEY ARE MOTHERS OF INDIVIDUAL FORMS.

The energies of God reside in different letters of the Sanskrit alphabets. The K group is the first group of consonants. There are other groups of consonants. There are also vowels, semi-vowels, and sibilants. Each of these groups contains different energies of God and various elements of creation. These letters are sounds, and are responsible for the creation of matter. They are mothers of individual forms because all matter is created by the energies of God residing in these different groups of letters. Ultimately, there is only one energy of God from which the other energies arise.

What this means is that all created matter is nothing but the energy of God. Different life forms may look different and may have different characteristics, but it is all composed of the same thing. Just as a cloth is nothing but thread, and a wave is nothing but water, in the same way the entire universe and every form in it is nothing but the energy of God. We may believe we are all separate from each other, but we are made up of the same energies of God. Thus, you can see the unity of existence. Many diverse life forms appear on the surface, but underlying all that is only the energy of God. When you change your belief and see only One Energy and not many forms, you are able to awaken from the illusion and experience Ultimate Reality.

triṣu caturthaṃ tailavad āsecyam

THE FOURTH STATE OF CONSCIOUSNESS SHOULD BE POURED LIKE OIL INTO THE OTHER THREE STATES.

The fourth state of consciousness is known as *turīya*, and it is a state of super-consciousness. The other three states are the waking state, the state of sleep with dreams, and the state of deep sleep where there are no dreams. The sutra is saying that one should bring the awareness you find in the fourth state, to the other three states also. In other words, one should remain aware in the other states too. This is similar to the eleventh sutra of the first chapter.

Initially, it is not possible to remain aware during the dream state and the state of deep sleep. One should start by being aware during the waking state. As our awareness grows, there will come a time when our awareness will never get 'switched off'. We will remain aware through all three states during the day and night. That is when we will become enlightened.

Oil changes the quality of any surface you pour it on. Even if you wipe the oil away, the surface continues to feel oily. Consciousness is like that. When you bring awareness into your life, it changes its quality in all the three states. During the waking state you become peaceful and happy, and in the two states of sleep, you rest deeply.

～ 21 ～

magnaḥ svacittena praviśet

BY FIXING THE MIND ON ONE'S OWN SELF, ONE MAY ENTER AND BE PLUNGED INTO HIGHER REALITY.

This sutra continues from the last sutra. It asks us to direct our attention to our own Self. Usually our attention is constantly directed outwards, to the external world. Now we are asked to direct some of that attention inwards, back towards the Self. We become agitated because the mind is focused on the external world, and the problems we are experiencing in our day-to-day lives. When we direct our attention to the Self, we immediately become peaceful.

Ramana Maharshi gave a beautiful example to explain this. He said it is hot under the sun and pleasant in the shade of the tree. A wise man does not leave the shade. Others, venture out, experience discomfort under the sun, and then come back into the shade. We do the same with the Self. Our mind leaves the Self, goes out into the world and experiences pain there. It then comes back to the Self, and experiences peace. The wise man is the one whose mind is constantly focused on the Self, and does not go back and forth between the Self and the external world. He also said that fixing the mind on the Self is the perfection of yoga, meditation, wisdom, and worship. All else is mere lecturing and pedantry.

If our mind is constantly focused on the Self, then how do we solve our problems, or tend to our work? Thomas Weiner once famously said, "Life resolves itself in the process of life itself." Each day life resolves some of our old problems, and brings new ones into our life. This process continues. It is not necessary to keep worrying about our problems. In fact, worrying does not find any solutions to our problems, and only damages our health. On the other hand, our Self or our Soul is the repository of the highest wisdom. The Self has much greater intelligence than the mind, and gives far better solutions for our problems. When we focus on the Self, we know intuitively what we need to do in that moment of our life. Accessing the soul's wisdom is the best thing we can do for facing the challenges in life.

The sutra says that we will be plunged into Higher Reality. It is trying to give us a sense of the vertical dimension. Normally, we live life on the horizontal plane. We are thinking of past, present, future, or planning linearly in terms of days, weeks, and months. Higher Reality brings us into the vertical plane. We suddenly move very deeply into the present moment. We are completely in the present moment, and there is not a single part of us that is in the past or the future. There is also a sense of depth about the present moment. We experience it very deeply.

prāṇa-samācāre samadarśanam

ON PRACTICING AWARENESS OF BREATH, THERE IS AN APPEARANCE OF ALL BEING THE SAME.

There are two popular meditations found in Kashmir Shaivism, involving the breath. One is to focus attention on the sound of one's breath. This is also known as so-hum meditation. Our in-breath makes the sound 'so', and our out-breath makes the sound 'hum'. The *Vigyan Bhairava Tantra* says that this meditation is easy to gain success with. It is difficult only for those who are not in their senses and are unable to practice it.

The second meditation given importance is focusing attention on the gap between two breaths. There is a gap between our in-breath and our out-breath, and another between our out-breath and our in-breath. The practice involves focusing on the breath, and the gap between two breaths.

An alternative method is simply to be aware of the breath, without focusing on the sound or the gap between breaths. This is the practice this sutra is probably referring to.

Practising breath awareness through any of the above methods is a very effective way of stilling the mind. It brings about rapid transformation. When the mind is stilled, we become liberated, and we experience all objects as same. They all appear the same because they are all made of the same energy. When we were living in the illusion, we were not able to see and experience that. When the veil is lifted, we see clearly.

~ **23** ~

Madhye 'vara-prasavaḥ

LOWER STATES OF BEING ARISE IN THE MIDDLE STAGES.

As mentioned earlier, there are four states of consciousness—the waking state, the dream state, the state of deep sleep, and the state of super consciousness or enlightenment. The middle stages is a reference to the middle of the first three states. When we are in the middle of the waking state, the dream state, or deep sleep, the level of awareness of an unenlightened person is low. This is why these middle stages are referred to as lower states of being, because there is less awareness there. However, at the beginning and end of the three states, during the crossover period, when one state is ending and another is beginning, it is possible to experience a heightened level of awareness. This crossover period is a time of great possibilities. Vasugupta explained this in verse 17 of the *Spanda Karikas*:

A fully enlightened person is constantly aware of his Self in the three transitory states. But others may find their Being at the beginning and end of these states.

It is difficult to be aware during the transition from the dream state to deep sleep because one is fully asleep. It is also not easy to be aware when sleep is ending and one is about to wake up, although it is possible to practise this at that time. The best time to try this is when one is about to fall asleep. When one is drifting into sleep, one should try and retain some awareness. When our state of consciousness shifts from one state to another, in that gap or junction point, it is possible to achieve enlightenment.

One has to try and maintain a balance. You cannot be completely aware while going to sleep because then you will be awake, and will not be able to sleep. On the other hand, if one loses awareness as one goes to sleep, then one will miss the junction point.

The *Vigyan Bhairava Tantra* also contains a meditation (verse 75) on the gap between two states:

Concentrate on the state where sleep has not fully appeared, but the external world has disappeared. In that state, the Supreme Goddess is revealed.

mātrā-svapratyaya-saṃdhāne naṣṭasya punarutthānam

ON BELIEVING FIRMLY THAT EVERYTHING IS ONE WITH ONE'S OWN SELF, THE HIGHEST STATE OF CONSCIOUSNESS THAT HAD DISAPPEARED, RISES AGAIN.

Our beliefs create our reality. Life responds to us depending on what we believe about it. If we believe the world is an evil place, events will occur to reconfirm that belief. If we believe the opposite, events will occur to reconfirm that too. If we believe making money is easy we will find no difficulty in earning money. One of the reasons we remain bound, is because we believe what our sense organs tell us. Our sense organs show that we live in a world with lots of different people and objects, and all these objects and people are separate from each other. They tell us that we are this limited body, and we have a particular name and identity. The reality is that none of this is true. We are not the body, we are consciousness. We are not something limited, we are infinite; and we are not separate, we are all one. The question now arises, how do we experience true reality? One way is to change our beliefs.

Incorrect beliefs have got us trapped in an incorrect reality. To rectify this, one has to rectify one's beliefs. One has to disregard the information being given by the sense organs. We should not go by appearances. In sutra 19 of this chapter, it was explained that all matter is created by God's energy. The same energy is in all of us, and in everything. Since we are all composed of the same energy, it means that in essence, we are this energy, and we are all one. (Energy comes from consciousness, so at a deeper level, we are all consciousness).

When we believe we are all one, our behaviour towards others changes completely. We treat them like we would treat ourselves. We no longer try and hurt others, as we would never try and hurt ourselves.

Believing we are all one causes a change in us at a much deeper level. Our desires become less, as we understand that all objects are made of the same thing. Diamonds are treated equally with objects of no monetary value. Ultimately, our mind becomes quieter, and our awareness grows till we reach the highest state of consciousness.

~੭ 25 ੮~

śiva-tulyo jāyate

ONE BECOMES EQUAL TO SHIVA.

The next few verses are about an enlightened person. An enlightened person becomes equal to Shiva, because an enlightened person *is* Shiva. There is only one Supreme Being, which in Shaivism is referred to as Shiva, in the Upanishads as Brahman, in other traditions as God, Ultimate Reality, and many other names. We are all part of this One Being. What enlightenment does is remove the veil and show us true reality. We see only One and not many, we see the depths of the ocean, not just the waves on the surface.

An enlightened person is one with Shiva and is a living embodiment of Shiva. It does not mean that the rest of us are not one with God. We are, but we are yet to experience our oneness with God. That is what liberation does to us. It makes us experience oneness, and not separation.

~ **26** ~

śarīravṛttir vratam

ONE REMAINS IN THE BODY TO SERVE.

An enlightened person can choose to stay in the body, or to leave. When they decide to stay on, it is usually because they choose to serve mankind. They have compassion for the suffering of humans and wish to show them a way out. This is also how you will recognize a true master. They do not ask to be served but are there to serve you. A recent example of this was Mother Teresa. It was her mission to help the poorest of the poor, those who had been abandoned by their families or by the society. She literally picked up people from the streets of Calcutta, who had been left to die because they had no family, or their family could not afford their medical expenses. She cared and looked after them in the last few moments of their lives, and showed them that they were still loved and not abandoned.

There are many masters like Mother Teresa who have continued to serve humanity. By their example they have shown the heights to which humans can rise to.

<hr>

~ 27 ~

katha japaḥ

HIS SPEECH IS A RECITATION OF PRAYER.

An enlightened master's speech is sacred because of the wisdom it contains. That is why it is considered a prayer. Usually after a master is gone, we strive to remember every word they said. Some of the famous masters' words are recorded in texts that have become sacred such as Lord Krishna's in the Bhagavad Gita, Buddha's in the Dhammapada, and Christ's in the New Testament of the Bible.

Sometimes, listening to a master's words is enough to stir something within us and bring about a transformation in our lives. Many find so much peace reading the speeches of Osho, Swami Vivekananda, Ramana Maharshi, and other masters. Each generation has living masters. People flock to hear them speak because of the knowledge and wisdom they impart.

~ 28 ~

dānam ātmajñānam

KNOWLEDGE OF THE SELF IS THE GIFT HE DISPENSES.

An enlightened person has reached the other shore. They have attained their highest Self. It is knowledge of this Self that they dispense to others. Because they are enlightened, they have knowledge and experience of the Ultimate Reality. They have experienced dimensions of life that we are completely unaware of. They try to describe their experiences in words, but words cannot do justice to the message they are trying to convey. This is because we do not have sufficient words to describe what they are experiencing. This is the reason why sometimes the words of masters are misunderstood. They are using limited words to convey experiences that are indescribable.

Take the example of a large room that is very dark. Someone brings a small candle in. With the light of the candle, we are faintly able to make out some of the objects in the room. But it is still mostly dark, and we can see very little. Now imagine, somebody puts on a switch, and the entire room is lit. We are able to clearly see everything that is in the room. A liberated person is like a lit room. Their inner light has been switched on, and they are now able to see Total Reality. We, on the other hand, are still groping in the dark. Now, the enlightened person tries to explain to us what they see, and some of their experiences may be initially difficult for us to understand. However, this is the gift they are giving us—knowledge of our higher Self, and knowledge of a higher reality.

yo 'vipastho jñāhetuśca

AND HE, WHO IS ESTABLISHED AS A RULER OF ENERGY, BECOMES A SOURCE OF WISDOM FOR OTHERS.

A liberated person is one who is established as a ruler of energy. They are a source of wisdom not just in spiritual matters but also in how to deal with problems in our day-to-day lives. Once Buddha was insulted by a man on the street. The person kept abusing him, but Buddha remained silent. Finally, the man got exasperated. Buddha then told him, "If you have a gift for someone, and that person does not accept the gift, then whom does the gift remain with?" The man then replied, "With me of course." Buddha then told him, it was the same with his abuse. If one does not accept another's abuse, the abuse remains with the person giving the abuse.

There is also the famous statement of Jesus Christ, "Do unto others, as you would have others do unto you." Christ had summarized the Law of Karma with this statement, and was giving very practical advice to his disciples on how to conduct their lives. Not only is this a very nice and ethical way to live, but it is also a practical way of life. As per the Law of Karma, whatever you do to others will be done to you, and whatever you fail to do for others, will fail to be done for you. This is because we are all one, and what goes around comes around. We think we are doing something to someone else, but actually we are doing it to ourselves. Sooner or later, we experience the fruits of our actions, whether they are good or bad. Whatever we cause someone else to experience, we will one day experience. If we bring happiness into someone's life, happiness will also be brought into our life. On the other hand, if we cheat someone, we will also be cheated sometime in the future.

These are just a few examples of how masters are a source of wisdom for others.

svaśakti-pracayo 'sya viśvam

THE UNIVERSE IS A COLLECTION
OF HIS OWN ENERGIES.

The universe is a collection of God's energies. An enlightened person is one with God, therefore the universe is also a collection of his or her energies. We are so used to thinking of separation, and believing that humans are separate from God and from each other, that we find it hard to believe that the universe could be a collection of some enlightened person's energies. The truth is that there is no separation, and there is only One Being (Shiva, God), that we are all a part of. The universe is composed of the energies of this One Being. Every object, every form in the universe is only a collection of God's energy in different combinations. Each object is a certain mix of God's energy.

~ 31 ~

sthiti-layau

HE CAN CHOOSE CONTINUED EXISTENCE OR DISSOLUTION OF THE BODY.

A liberated person has completed the cycle of birth and death. They have attained the pinnacle of what a human can reach. They have realized their true self, and have awakened from the illusion. There is nothing else for them to do; they have achieved all that they came here to achieve. Now, they have a choice. They can continue to remain in the body, or they can leave the body. If they remain in the body, it is usually because they wish to serve humanity, and help others in their evolution. If they decide to stay on, their influence continues for several years after the ultimate death of their body. Their teachings may survive for many centuries after their death, as has happened with the great masters. People also go on pilgrimages to the important places where they lived or taught during their lifetime. Some of these places have a special energy, which can be experienced centuries after the masters have passed away.

tat pravṛttau api anirāsaḥ saṃvetṛ-bhāvāt

IN EITHER EVENT, BECAUSE HE IS IN THE ALL-KNOWING STATE, HE REMAINS IN THAT STATE.

After liberation, a master is omniscient and is in the all-knowing state. Whether he chooses to continue in the body, or to leave the body, he remains in the all-knowing state. If he chooses to leave the body, he continues to exist in another plane of existence, and he remains in the all-knowing state. If he chooses to stay in the body, he also continues to remain in the all-knowing state. Liberation cannot be reversed. Once you reach that state you remain there, irrespective of whether you choose to remain in the body or not.

sukha-duḥkhayor bahirmananam

PLEASURE AND PAIN ARE CONSIDERED TO BE SOMETHING EXTERNAL.

To a liberated person, pleasure and pain are experienced as something external. This is because they no longer identify with the body. The body is seen as something different from them. Pleasure and pain is something that happens to the body and not to them, that is why it is experienced as something external, and not as something they are experiencing.

The rest of us still very strongly identify with the body. To us, pleasure and pain seem very real because our awareness has not reached the level where we can disconnect with the body. It is for this reason we spend most of our lives seeking pleasures and avoiding pain. Tantra says, this is one of the causes of suffering in our lives. Pleasure and pain are unavoidable. They are a cycle like day and night. It is impossible to have one without the other. Yet we spend most of our lives chasing one and avoiding the other. This is the reason we try to acquire more money. We believe with greater wealth we can have more pleasures and less pain. Tantra says, this is not true. Pain is unavoidable and greater wealth does not reduce our chances of experiencing pain.

However, pain does not have to cause suffering. Suffering is due to our thought about pain. We believe pain is bad, pain should not be happening to us, and our negative thoughts about pain cause us suffering. Non-acceptance of pain leads to suffering. On the other hand, experiencing pain without passing judgment on it eliminates suffering. An experience is simply what it is, whether it is pleasure, pain, or anything else. When we think about it and pass judgment on it, we open ourselves to the possibility of an event affecting us emotionally and causing us happiness or making us suffer. When we experience events with awareness and without passing judgment, we remain peaceful, irrespective of whether the event is pleasurable or painful.

Ultimately, when our awareness grows to the level when we no longer identify with the body, then the entire cycle of pain and pleasure is viewed as something external. It is experienced as happening 'outside', to someone else, not to us. There are some masters like Ramana Maharshi, whose bodies died of cancer. They should have experienced great pain towards the end of their lives when cancer enveloped their body, but they felt none of it. They were completely disconnected with the body, and what was happening to the body no longer affected them.

❧ 34 ❧

tadvimuktastu kevali

FREE OF THEM, THEN, THE LIBERATED STATE WHERE THERE IS ONLY ONE.

When you are free of being affected by pleasures and pain, it means you have reached the liberated state. There is a word used in the sutra, *kevali*, which is not so simple to translate into English. A literal translation of the sutra would be, **Free of them, then, Kevali**. Kevali is a state of liberation. It is also translated as alone, aloneness, one. In the state of liberation, you are alone because there is only you, there is only One that exists. In the liberated state, there are not many, there is only One. We think of all the liberated masters, and sometimes believe that they must be in some special place called heaven. Actually, they are all in the same place because they are all one. Liberation causes you to experience oneness. There is only God, and God is alone.

So, kevali gives you the sense of being liberated and being alone. You are all there is in the universe. This is easier to understand when we use the word God. God is all there is and God is alone. After enlightenment, we become one with God, and experience ourselves as God. Our sense of being an individual disappears completely.

Vasugupta explained in the *Spanda Karikas* that when you understand that everything comes from the same source, you will not be troubled by another person. There are some people we believe harass us and cause us pain. When we realize at a deeper level that we are one with them, they cease to affect us emotionally.

mohapratisaṃhatas tu karmātmā

BUT ONE WHO IS SHRUNK BY DELUSION BELIEVES THE SELF PERFORMS ACTIONS.

Ignorance or delusion shrinks our sense of self. It makes us forget our bigger self, the self that is one with God, and causes us to believe we are the little self, the body. The body performs actions, and we believe we are the body, this individual performing all these activities. We become concerned with the achievements of the body. We strive for a good education, to amass wealth, to gain recognition and success in our worldly life; and towards the end of our life, we become fearful when death approaches.

All this while we forget about our bigger self, our soul. Our soul is the witness within us that observes the ups and downs in our life. It is not interested in the success and failures of the body, and nor is it concerned about the death of the body. As Vasugupta beautifully explains in the *Spanda Karikas* (Verses 14-16):

Two are found to exist here, called the Creator and the created. Among them, created matter is subject to decay but the Creator is imperishable.

Looking at created matter dissolving into the whole, examine carefully what is being destroyed here. At the time of his death, an ignorant man thinks, "I will cease to exist".

But the Being within us, who is the abode of the quality of omniscience, cannot be destroyed. Due to lack of knowledge of this other Self, a man believes sooner or later, he may cease to exist.

Ignorance or delusion causes us to forget our real Self and makes us believe we are the body.

bheda-tiraskāre
sargāntara-karmatvam

ON THE DISAPPEARANCE OF DIFFERENCE, ONE GAINS THE ABILITY TO CREATE ANOTHER WORLD.

After enlightenment, there is disappearance of difference. We no longer see difference and separation; we experience oneness. At this stage, we gain the ability to create another world. The passage from Vasugupta's *Spanda Karikas* quoted above states that two are found to exist here—the Creator and the created. Before enlightenment we believe we are the body or created matter. After enlightenment we realize we are one with God, we are one with the Creator. There is a shift from thinking we are created matter to becoming the Creator. When we become the Creator (i.e. become one with God), we can create a whole new world, or many new worlds.

The sutras describe some amazing things an enlightened person can do. They are able to do this because they are one with God, and God has the power to do these things. However, it should be understood that an enlightened person is fully merged with God. They have no sense of ego or selfish desire left. They would, therefore, not use their powers for the fulfilment of any egotistical desires, as there is no ego left. They have no independent will. They have become God in human form. What is God's will is their will. The possibility of misuse of these powers for personal gain does not exist, as there is no person or individual left.

~ **37** ~

karaṇaśaktiḥ svato 'nubhavāt

ONE HAS THE POWER TO CREATE FROM ONE'S OWN EXPERIENCE.

This sutra continues from the last sutra. One has the ability to create from one's own experience. The word experience is used here in a broader sense. It conveys that one can create from the knowledge and power inherent in oneself. This sutra is repeating what was said in sutra 17 of this chapter—one can create from one's own self.

The power to create is there within each of us. Even before enlightenment, we are creating events in our life through our thoughts, words, and deeds. However, the power to create is fully realized only after enlightenment, when we become one with our Creator.

~ **38** ~

tripad ādy anuprāṇanam

AFTER ENLIGHTENMENT, THERE IS AN INFUSION OF VITALITY, BEGINNING WITH THE THREE STATES.

Enlightenment brings about a complete change in the energy within us. A rise in our level of consciousness is also accompanied by a rise in our level of energy. The energy Kundalini, which is dormant within us, has risen from the root chakra to the highest chakra. This energy vitalizes our body and the three states of consciousness. The three states of consciousness—the waking state, the dream state, and the state of deep sleep—are now infused with the energy of the fourth state, the state of super consciousness.

The energy of the fourth state completely revitalizes the other three states. In the waking state, a liberated person has a lot more energy to complete the work they wish to do during the day. They also require fewer hours of sleep. During sleep, our soul again experiences the joy of oneness with God. That is why sleep refreshes us. It is a state of unity with God but without awareness. However, the soul of an enlightened person is constantly experiencing the joy of unity with God, during sleep and during the waking hours. They therefore require fewer hours of sleep because they are constantly infused with the joy and energy of God, in all the three states of existence.

cittasthitivat śarīra-karaṇa-bāhyeṣu

AS IN THE STATES OF MIND, SO ALSO IN THE BODY, THE SENSE ORGANS, AND IN EXTERIOR ACTIONS.

Our body is nothing but an energy system. All matter is created by energy and is composed of energy. When we become ill, it means the energy flow in our body has been disturbed. Some parts of our body are not getting adequate energy. That is why some eastern systems of healing, such as acupuncture, try to balance the flow of energy in our body to cure illness.

With enlightenment, the dormant energy in our body has awakened. This energy vitalizes not just the three states of consciousness but also our entire body. Every inch of our body, every sense organ, every internal organ gets vitalized by this energy. Enlightenment brings about an entire transformation of the body. Various ailments and illnesses disappear. Some of the effects of aging are reversed. This does not mean that the body becomes immortal; it does not. But the body gets a new lease of life. The body becomes healthier and feels younger than what it was before enlightenment.

Sometimes, even a near death experience (NDE) is sufficient to transform and heal the body. There was the recent case of Anita Moorjani, who was dying from cancer. She was in the final stages of cancer and slipped into a coma. The doctors had given up on her, and felt it was only a matter of time before she passed away. During her coma, Anita had a near death experience, and passed to the other realm for a short period of time. She came back from her NDE and awoke from her coma. The insights she received during her NDE transformed her completely. Her cancer went into remission, and within a few short weeks, she was completely free of this disease. She described her experiences in her bestselling book *Dying To Be Me*.

Her doctors wondered what flicked the switch on. What caused the cancer to suddenly reverse and go into remission? When our consciousness rises to another level, it has an immediate positive effect on the body.

~ **40** ~

abhilāṣād bahirgatiḥ saṃvāhyasya

DUE TO DESIRE MOVING OUTWARDS FOR EXTERNAL OBJECTS, AN INDIVIDUAL IS CARRIED FROM LIFE TO LIFE.

One of the reasons we are reborn is that we still have desires that are unfulfilled. There is something we still wish to achieve, some object we wish to acquire, or some experience we wish to have that is causing us to be reborn. These desires have to do with the external world. They are not desires for our spiritual progress, or for self-realization, which are internal in nature.

Desire is a very powerful creative force. Life conspires to bring us what we desire. Some people may feel that this cannot be true because most of their desires never get fulfilled. The fastest way to fulfil a desire is to keep choosing the same thing. Many people keep changing their mind about what they choose. Some of our strong desires remain unfulfilled in our lifetime. This causes us to be reborn, so that those desires can be fulfilled in another lifetime.

Does this mean that all desires are bad and cause rebirth? No, generally a desire will reflect on the size of the ego. When the ego is strong, the desires will reflect that, and will be for personal fame and grandeur. When our awareness grows, our sense of ego and individuality diminish, and our desires will reflect that. They will be more for the general good than for individual grandeur. The desires being discussed in this sutra are those that show you still have an ego left.

There is also a difference between desires that are addictions and those that are preferences. A desire is an addiction when we become unhappy in case the desire does not get fulfilled. A preference is when we prefer a particular outcome, but are not unhappy in case that does not materialize. Ken Keyes Jr. and Neale Donald Walsch both taught that the way to mastery is to elevate our desires from addictions to preferences. Don't be addicted to a particular result, prefer a particular result. Next, elevate your preferences to acceptance. Accept what shows up. When we are able to do this, our desires no longer cause rebirth. This is what Lord Krishna also taught in the Bhagavad Gita. He said, don't be addicted to results. Work for the sake of work, not for the end result.

Ken Keyes' life was a living demonstration of this truth. He also taught that external circumstances were not the source of our happiness, but our inner reaction to them. When people went for his talks, they were shocked to see that he was on a wheelchair. Yet, he was so happy and spoke with such joy of life. He explained that if he had been addicted to greater mobility, he would never have been happy. But he had elevated his desire for mobility to the level of preference, which is why he could be happy even though he was on a wheelchair. This is the way to mastery. Change addictions to preferences, and change preferences to acceptance.

〜 **41** 〜

tadārūḍhapramites tatkṣayāj jīvasaṃkṣayaḥ

FROM DESTRUCTION OF DESIRE, ONE RISES TO THE LIBERATED STATE AND THERE IS COMPLETE DISAPPEARANCE OF THE INDIVIDUAL.

When desire is completely destroyed, or raised to the level of acceptance, then at that time, one rises to the liberated state. In the liberated state, there is complete merger with God and there is no trace of the individual.

Desire can be one of the root causes of unhappiness in our life. Sometimes we become fixated on achieving a certain amount of success. We want to be a 'somebody'. We become disappointed if life does not turn out the way we wanted. We may even become bitter or depressed about our life situation. At that time, it is important to remember the wisdom of the sutras given in the beginning of this chapter, and also remember what Shakespeare said—we are like actors on a stage. We are playing a role in life, and we should not make that role real.

We may be a successful lawyer or a failed lawyer, a successful businessman or a complete failure as a businessman. In either event, that is not really who we are. Our role in life is completely separate from our Self or our Soul. When you can stand back and observe your life, and understand that none of it is real, then you can truly enjoy life. You will be able to laugh at some of your failures and misfortunes, and understand there is a lot you can learn from them.

～ 42 ～

bhūta-kañcukī tadā vimukto bhūyaḥ patisamaḥ paraḥ

THEN, THE BODY MADE OF ELEMENTS IS ONLY
A COVER, AND BEING LIBERATED, ONE IS
SUPREME, IDENTICAL TO THE LORD.

In the liberated state, there is no identification or attachment with the body. The body, made of the gross elements, is like a cover over our true self. There is complete unification with God, and that is why one is identical to the Lord. A few of the earlier sutras had described some amazing things an enlightened person could do. They are all able to do this because they became identical to Shiva or God. There is no difference or separation between them and God, and the powers they have are the powers God has. They have become God in human form.

❧ **43** ❧

naisargikaḥ prāṇasaṃbandhaḥ

THE BOND OF THE LIFE FORCE WITH THE BODY IS NATURAL.

If the body is only a cover, then why is the body required after one is liberated? Will the body not waste away or cease to exist after liberation? It is to answer these questions that this sutra has been given. Even though the body is only a cover, the bond or attachment of the life force with the body is natural. Liberation does not cause destruction of the body. In fact, liberation improves the health of the body because the life force is now fully awakened in the body. This is fully explained above in sutra 39.

However, after liberation, one has a choice whether to continue in the body, or leave the body (sutra 31). The decision of when to leave the body is always taken at the level of the soul. Those of us who are not liberated are not usually in touch with our soul, which is why we cannot predict the date of the passing away of our body. On the other hand, an awakened master is one with the soul. They can choose to remain in the body or leave it.

nāsikā-antarmadhya-saṃyamāt kimatra savyāpasavya-sau-ṣumneṣu

FROM CONCENTRATING THE MIND AT THE CENTRE IN THE MIDDLE OF THE NOSE, THERE, AT THE MEETING POINT OF THE LEFT, RIGHT, AND CENTRAL CHANNELS, ONE IS LIBERATED.

In the second-last sutra, one final meditation is being given which can liberate us. The centre in the middle of the nose is the eyebrow centre. It is a special place because it is the front part of Ajna chakra, the second highest chakra. Ajna chakra is also important because three major channels join there. According to the physiology of yoga, the body has seventy-two thousand channels (nadis) through which energy flows in the body. Out of seventy-two thousand, three are most important—the left channel (*Ida Nadi*), the right channel (*Pingala Nadi*), and the central channel (*Sushumna Nadi*).

The central channel starts from the base chakra (Muladhara), and rises vertically through the spine. All chakras are located within this channel. The left and right channels also start from the base chakra and move upwards in a semi-circular manner. They move in opposite directions and crisscross each other in every chakra. The left channel moves left and upwards from the base chakra, in a semi-circular path. It starts left, and then comes back right till it meets the second chakra, Svadhishthana chakra. It then crosses the second chakra, moves right, and then circles back left to the third chakra, Manipura. The right channel moves in the opposite direction to the left channel. From the base chakra the right channel starts right, and then circles back left to the second chakra. It passes through the second chakra, moves left, and circles back right to the third chakra.

All three channels meet at the six main chakras. The central channel rises vertically, and the other two channels crisscross each other in a semi-circular path. The left and right channel finally end at Ajna chakra, the sixth chakra and the second highest chakra. Both these channels meet the central channel at Ajna chakra. From there, only one channel proceeds directly upwards to Sahasrara chakra, at the crown of the head.

The eyebrow centre, the front part of Ajna Chakra, is the final meeting point of the three channels or pathways. This sutra asks us to meditate on this point. We are to direct our attention to the eyebrow centre. Usually, this is practiced with our eyes closed. The practice of gazing at the eyebrow centre is called *Shambhavi Mudra*. A mudra is a posture of pose that changes the energy flow in the body. They usually bring about a heightened level of awareness. Shambhavi Mudra is one of the most powerful mudras. Staring at the eyebrow centre automatically quietens the mind. The eyebrow centre, for some reason, has a very powerful effect on the mind. When we direct our attention there, the mind starts becoming silent. When it falls completely silent, we are liberated.

Lord Krishna also recommends this meditation in the Bhagavad Gita (6:10-13):

Staying alone in a secluded place,
free from desires and unnecessary possessions,
the yogi should constantly apply himself
in controlling the mind with the Self.

The yogi should seat himself in a
clean place that is stable,
neither too high nor too low and
is covered first with grass,
then with a deer or tiger skin,
followed by a piece of cloth.

Sitting down at that place, he should practice yoga
for purification of the Self.
There, to control thoughts and the activities of the senses,
fix the attention of the mind on one object.

Maintaining an erect body, neck and head,
that is still and immobile,
look at the top of one's own nose (the eyebrow center),
and do not look in any other direction.

～ **45** ～

bhūyaḥ syāt pratimīlanam

ONE MAY RETURN FROM THE UN-AWAKENED STATE AND BE A GREATER SELF ONCE AGAIN.

The sutras end with an invitation—an invitation to awaken from the dream state and be a greater Self once again. The elements of concealment have drawn a veil over our true Self, and made us believe we are the body. However, this is not our natural state, and we can return to our true state when we choose to. The key element in making this happen is to have the desire to be whole again. It is our desire for liberation that sets this process into motion. That is what this sutra is inviting us to do—choose to be a greater Self once again.

The seventy-seven sutras have given us a great deal of wisdom. Now, we are invited to awaken and return to the infinite peace and bliss of our true Self. That is what this text has been about—to show us how to be a greater Self once again.

Bibliography

Byrom, Thomas. 1990, 2001. *The Heart of Awareness: A Translation of the Ashtavakra Gita.* Boston: Shambhala.

Chatterjee, Jagadish Chandra. 1914, 2009. *Kashmir Shaivism: A brief Introduction to the History, Literature and Shaiva Philosophy of Kashmir.* India: Gulshan Books.

Chaudhri, Ranjit. 2011. *112 Meditations For Self Realization: Vigyan Bhairava Tantra.* India: Prakash Books India Pvt. Ltd.

Dyczkowski, Mark S. G. 1992. *The Aphorisms of Shiva.* USA: State University of New York Press.

Lakshmanjoo, Swami. 2002. *Shiva Sutras: The Supreme Awakening.* USA: Universal Shaiva Fellowship.

Maharaj, Sri Nisargadatta. 1973, 2003. *I Am That.* India: Chetana (P) Ltd.

Maharshi, Sri Ramana. 1969, 1996. *Words of Grace.* Tiruvannamalai: Sri Ramanasramam.

Mascaro, Juan. 1962, 1994. The Bhagavad Gita. England: Penguin Books Ltd.

Mascaro, Juan. 1965, 1981. The Upanishads. England: Penguin Books Ltd.

Moorjani, Anita. 2012, 2013. *Dying To Be Me.* India: Hayhouse Publishers (India) Pvt. Ltd.

Mukherjee, Radhakamal. *Astavakragita* (The Song of the Self Supreme). India: Motilal Banarsidass Publishers Private Limited, 1971, 2000.

Radhakrishnan, S. *The Principal Upanishads.* India: Harper Collins Publishers India, 1994, 1997.

Saraswati, Swami Niranjanananda. 2013. *Tantra Darshan.* Munger, India: Yoga Publications Trust.

Singh, Jaideva. 1979, 2000. *Siva Sutras.* Delhi: Motilal Banarsidass Publishers Private Limited

Singh, Jaideva. 1980, 2000. *Spanda Karikas.* Delhi: Motilal Banarsidass Publishers Private Limited.

Venkataramiah, Mungala. 1955, 2000. *Talks with Sri Ramana Maharshi.* Tiruvannamalai: Sri Ramanasramam.

Walsch, Neale Donald. 1999. *Conversations with God: Book 3, An Uncommon Dialogue*. Great Britain: Hodder and Stoughton.

Walsch, Neale Donald. 1999. *Friendship With God: An Uncommon Dialogue*. Great Britain: Hodder and Stoughton

Yogananda, Sri Sri Paramahansa. *God Talks With Arjuna: The Bhagavad Gita*. Kolkata: Yogoda Satsanga Society of India, 2002.

1974. The Holy Bible, King James Version. New York: New American Library.

The Sutras

Chapter One

1. The Self is Consciousness.
2. Knowledge causes bondage.
3. The origin of this group is the elements that cause identification with the body.
4. Matrika governs this knowledge.
5. Vigorous and continuous effort leads to God.
6. On uniting the energy in the chakras, the universe ceases to exist.
7. On differentiating oneself from the body in the waking state, the dream state, and the state of deep sleep, one enjoys the birth of the fourth state.
8. The waking state consists of knowledge of the external world.

9. The dream state is a variety of imaginings.

10. There is no awareness in the illusory state of deep sleep.

11. One who experiences this triad is the chief of heroes.

12. The different stages of yoga cause amazement.

13. The power of desire is the Goddess, consort of Shiva.

14. The entire world is one's own body.

15. From focusing the mind on the heart, the world appears as a dream.

16. Or from joining with the Pure State, one obtains Divine Energy.

17. Deliberation leads to knowledge of the Self.

18. The joy of liberation is bliss for the whole world.

19. On uniting with Energy, one gains the ability to leave the body.

20. One has the power to join elements, or to separate elements, or to join everything.

21. Through the appearance of pure knowledge, one attains mastery of the chakras.

22. From union with the great lake, one gains the power of Mantra.

Chapter Two

1. Mantra stills the mind.
2. Persevering effort leads to fulfilment.
3. Knowledge on the reality of the body is the secret of mantra.
4. In the interior of the active mind is found inferior knowledge of the dream world.
5. On raising of knowledge inherent in oneself, one reaches the highest state of consciousness, which is the state of Shiva.
6. The Guru is the means.
7. For awakening the energy in the chakras.
8. The body is the sacrifice.
9. Knowledge is food to be consumed.
10. On destruction of this knowledge, one awakens from experiencing the dream state.

Chapter Three

1. The individual self is the mind.
2. Knowledge causes bondage.
3. The illusion is caused by the inability to discern the nature of elements, beginning with the elements of concealment.
4. Dissolution of the elements of concealment in the body leads to,
5. Suspension of breath in the channels, control over the elements, detachment from the elements, and separation from the elements.
6. Supernatural powers are due to a veil drawn by delusion.
7. From a complete and all-pervasive victory over delusion, one gains the victory of natural, innate knowledge of True Reality.
8. Becoming awake is the second effect.
9. The self is an actor.
10. The inner self is the stage.
11. The sense organs are the spectators.
12. Through desire for spiritual wisdom, one attains the True State.
13. Freedom is acquired.

14. Since there, so elsewhere.
15. Attentiveness is the seed.
16. Sitting comfortably, one effortlessly dives into an ocean of bliss.
17. He can bring about creation of matter from his own self.
18. When knowledge of Self becomes permanent, the possibility of another birth is completely eliminated.
19. Maheshwari and other energies of God, reside in the letters beginning with the K group, and they are mothers of individual forms.
20. The fourth state of Consciousness should be poured like oil into the other three states.
21. By fixing the mind on one's own Self, one may enter and be plunged into Higher Reality.
22. On practicing awareness of breath, there is an appearance of all being the same.
23. Lower states of being arise in the middle stages.
24. On believing firmly that everything is one with one's own self, the highest state of consciousness that had disappeared, rises again.
25. One becomes equal to Shiva.
26. One remains in the body to serve.

27. His speech is a recitation of prayer.

28. Knowledge of the Self is the gift he dispenses.

29. And he, who is established as a ruler of energy, becomes a source of wisdom for others.

30. The universe is a collection of his own energies.

31. He can choose continued existence or dissolution of the body.

32. In either event, because he is in the all-knowing state, he remains in that state.

33. Pleasure and pain are considered to be something external.

34. Free of them, then, the liberated state where there is only One.

35. But one who is shrunk by delusion believes the self performs actions.

36. On the disappearance of difference, one gains the ability to create another world.

37. One has the power to create from one's own experience.

38. After enlightenment, there is an infusion of vitality, beginning with the three states.

39. As in the states of mind, so also in the body, the sense organs, and in exterior actions.

40. Due to desire moving outwards for external objects, an individual is carried from life to life.

41. From destruction of desire, one rises to the liberated state and there is complete disappearance of the individual.

42. Then, the body made of elements is only a cover, and being liberated, one is Supreme, identical to the Lord.

43. The bond of the life force with the body is natural.

44. From concentrating the mind at the centre in the middle of the nose, there, at the meeting point of the left, right, and central channels, one is liberated.

45. One may return from the un-awakened state and be a greater Self once again.